Inspirational Thoughts...

Journal Book

not just for **Girlfriends**

by Linda H. Williams
with Angie CJ Sims

DEDICATED TO

My Parents ~ My History

Rev. & Mrs. John T. Hilliard

My Sons ~ My Legacy

Emory & Raphael

What People Are Saying

Thank you for sharing your insights to remind us of what is the truth.   ~ Eileen Foster

Thank you so much for all your positive posts. You are amazing and I truly appreciate you.   ~Sabriyah Smith

I look forward to your posts everyday.   ~LaMarr Smith

Your inspirational thoughts are provoking, on point, encouraging and uplifting. There are times when your thoughts come right on time, at a moment when I need a word. It's refreshing and a blessing.   ~Vanessa Austin

When I read your thoughts, it's like you wrote that just for me. It's what I needed to hear. You are a blessing to all! Thank you for sharing.   ~ Susie Williams

Your inspirational thoughts are very encouraging to me. It prepares me for the positive as well as the negative as I go about my day. Please keep them coming. ~ Donna Hayes

Very uplifting.   ~ Pamela Schiavone

Sometimes it's just the bit of encouragement that I need.
                                                                  ~Dr. Tyra Wingo

As a fellow believer, I find your posts encouraging and refreshing among all the hate and divisiveness among us.
                                                                  ~Veronica Holder

When I read your inspirational thoughts, it's like they can see what I am going through and are meant for me.
~Dennis J. Huebner

I read your inspirations daily, even though I might not need that word of encouragement right then, when circumstances arise, the right inspiration always comes to mind.
~ Faney Foster

Your inspirational thoughts are always a great way to stay uplifted and inspired. The message always resonates with my spirit. Always very timely. Much love.
~ Dora Chambers

Kind, loving, honest, respectful and reassuring.
~Anita Vitale Dudas

I always have a pen handy. Always hits my heart and opens my mind.
~ Melissa Moncree Secka

Your inspirational thoughts are always right on time. The reflection they provide helps to understand what the spirit is trying to get us to receive. I always feel like you're talking only to me…Thank you sis for your words and heart.
~Monique Scott

Let me start by saying that you are a very inspirational person. You inspire and motive me in ways to keep going, keep breathing, keep knowing that I, Natasha, will get there. Thank you, Ms. Linda for all your inspirational words. Don't stop.
~Natasha Ballantyne Alexander

It's always what I needed to hear, very encouraging and blessing to my daily life. Thank you for always inspiring me to listen to my inner voice. You're a motivator to us all. Keep your ministry going   ~Tracy T. Eghan

I love the inspiring and positive uplifting of your inspirational thoughts. They are always on point. Keep up the great work in sharing your words. God has guided you to share your talents and blessings with others.

~Wanda Pearson

I love the idea of what you have committed to do. God is good always and will forever be in the midst of that which is ordained   ~ Nikki Ruffin Smith

I look forward to your inspirational thoughts. I love truth and authenticity and that's what I get when reading your words. May God continue to drop nuggets into your spirit that will continue to bless others.   ~Lolitha Terry

Thank you

SPECIAL THANK YOU

VANESSA R. AUSTIN

MICHELE CARSON

SOUL DANCER

DR. JERRICA DODD

EVIE FLEMING

NADINE GREEN

VICKI POOLE

RAVON POOLE

A personal journal is an ideal environment in which to "BECOME." It is a perfect place for you to think, feel, discover, expand, remember and dream.

–Brad Wilcox

PREFACE

It was suggested to me approximately five (5) years ago that I should begin to increase my social presence. It was for that initial purpose that I started posting my *Inspirational Thoughts.* God had another purpose in mind.

In 1991, I attended a vision board party and one of my goals was to have an international platform. Over the years, I have received comments from as far away as Dubai, Australia and South Africa from people who have been personally touched and affected by a word that I shared. I speak from a platform of hope, empowerment and restoration and the Lord answered my prayers for that international platform to spread this message. Although my ministry is primarily for women, my message is not gender specific.

The sole purpose of this journal is to encourage you as you travel through this journey called life. Writing your thoughts, emotions, and how you're coping with life's challenges, often provides a release.

We are blessed to be a blessing to someone else. If God has blessed you, and if you're reading this, He has, spread the love. *"When the Praises go up. the Blessings come down!"*

Be blessed

Linda H. Williams

Day 1

Life becomes easier when you learn to accept an apology you never got. ~Robert Brault

Day 2

Be grateful for the good times and keep the faith during the bad times. Stay positive when life gives you every reason to be negative.

~ Truthfollower.com

Day 3

The difference between stumbling blocks and stepping stones is how you use them.

~ Author Unknown

Day 4

Everyday is a second chance.
~ Fabquote.com

Day 5

Respect yourself enough to walk away from anything that no longer serves you, grows you or makes you happy. ~ Robert Tew

Day 6

One of the happiest moments in life is when you find the courage to let go of what you cannot change.

~ EmilysQuotes

Day 7

The consequences of today are determined by the actions of the past. To change the future, you must alter your decisions today.
~ S. N. Goenka

Day 8

When things aren't adding up in your life, start subtracting. ~ Bruce Van Horn

Day 9

The unselfish effort to bring cheer to others will be the beginning of a happier life for yourself.
~ Helen Keller

Day 10

You've got to think about big things while you're doing small things, so that all the small things go in the right direction.

~ Alvin Toffler

Day 11

Live your life for you and not for anyone else. Don't let the fear of being rejected, judged, or disliked stop you from being yourself.
~ *Sonya Parker*

Day 12

Life has no remote. Get up and change it yourself.

~ Mark A. Cooper

Day 13

Embrace the seasons of your life, for it is just that…a season.   ~ Women In The Mix

Day 14
When you focus on problems, you'll have more problems. When you focus on possibilities, you'll have more opportunities.

~ Zig Ziglar

Day 15

How you think determines how you act. How you act in turn determines how others react to you. ~ David J. Schwartz

Day 16

If you do not know your own worth and value, don't expect someone else to calculate it for you. ~ *Themindsjournal.com*

Day 17

Never apologize for being you. Others should apologize for asking you to be something else.   ~ Adapted from Curiano.com

Day 18 *Even your past pain can be a blessing to someone. Hope lifters are willing to reach back and pass hope on. ~ Unknown Author*

Day 19

Stop complaining about things you are not willing to change. ~ *Pinterest*

Day 20

You can make the world a better place by making yourself a better person.
~ Scott Sorrell

Day 21

Fill your life with experiences not things. Have stories to tell, not stuff to show.

~ Pinterest.com

Day 22 *Happiness is not something you postpone for the future. It's something you design for the present.* ~ *Jim Rohn*

Day 23

It may not be time to close the book-just time to turn the page. Don't give up on your dream.   ~Adapted from Amy Rees Anderson

Day 24

Where you are today is the result of decisions you made yesterday. If you want your tomorrow to be different than your today, you must begin to make better decisions.

~ Linda H. Williams

Day 25

The more you thank life, the more life gives you to be thankful for.
~ Unknown Author

Day 26
Pursuit of excellence is gratifying and healthy. The pursuit of perfection is frustrating, neurotic and a waste of time.
~ Edwin Bliss

Day 27

Don't lose yourself in the process of holding onto someone who doesn't care about losing you.

~ Quotesvalley.com

Day 28

It all begins with you. If you do not care for yourself, you will not be strong enough to take care of anything or anyone in life.
~ Leon Brown

Day 29

I hope you are living a life that you are proud of. If you find you're not, I hope you have the strength to start all over again.

~ F. Scott Fitzgerald

____

____

____

____

____

____

____

____

____

____

Day 30
Your condition is not your conclusion. Don't mistake your journey for your destination.

~ Adapted from Kendrick L. Meredith Sr.

Day 31

Ignore negative people. They feed on your reaction and if they see you being affected by what they do or say, they'll keep doing it.

~ Pinterest.com

Day 32

Be more concerned with your character than your reputation because your character is what you really are while your reputation is merely what others think you are.

~ John Wooden

Day 33

Sometimes in life, we make the mistake of giving certain people the places which they never deserve in our life.   ~ Luckybannu

Day 34

Day 35   *Confidence is something you create within yourself by believing in who you are.*
~ Wisdomhealingcenter.com

Day 36

If you live for the applause of other people, you will also live in the fear of their disapproval.

~ Mat Kearney

Day 37

Don't ever change just to impress someone. Change because it makes you a better person and leads to a better future.

~ Livelifehappy.com

Day 38

If you continue to do the same things you have always done, you will continue to get the same results you have always gotten. So, ask yourself, are you satisfied with who you are?
~ Adapted from boardofwisdom.com

Day 39

You have to learn to say no without feeling guilty. Setting boundaries is healthy. You need to learn to respect and take care of yourself.

~ Friendsloveforever.com

Day 40

Let go of those who bring you down and surround yourself with those who bring out the best in you. ~ Unknown/Boardofwisdom.com

____

____

____

____

____

____

____

____

____

Day 41

Be careful how you talk to yourself. Your internal conversations are on-going and you are listening. What are you saying about yourself? ~ *Adapted from Lisa M. Hayes*

Day 42

To be beautiful means to be you. You don't need to be accepted by others. You just need to accept yourself. What do you see when you look in the mirror?

~ Adapted from Thich Nhat Hahn

Day 43

Some people are like clouds in your life. When they go away, it's always a brighter day.

~ Author Unknown

Day 44

Happiness is the joy you feel on your way to your full potential.

~ Adapted from Shawn Achor

Day 45   *When you fall, don't look where you fell, look where you slipped.   ~ African Proverb*

Day 46

When asked if my cup is half full or half empty, my response was I'm thankful that I have a cup. ~ Linda H. Williams

Day 47

The only keeper of your happiness is you. Stop giving people power to control your smile, your worth and your attitude.
~ *Mandy Hale*

Day 48

Some people pass through our lives for a season to teach us lessons that could never be learned if they stayed. ~ Mandy Hale

Day 49   *If you want light to come into your life, you must stand where it is shining.*

~ Guy Finley

Day 50

Being with no one is better than being with the wrong one. Sometimes, those who fly solo have the strongest wings.

~ Livelifehappy.com

Day 51

Your mind is like a garden. Your thoughts are the seeds. You can grow flowers or you can grow weeds.   ~ *Pinterest.com*

Day 52   *Good things come to those who wait but the best things come to those who work for it.*
~ Thegoodvibe.com

Day 53
While most people know that life is a journey, they still choose to drive on autopilot.

~ Mark Desvaux

Day 54

Your value doesn't decrease based on someone's inability to see your worth.

~ Ted Rubin

Day 55   *Never put the key to your happiness in someone else's pocket. ~ Wisdomquotes4u.com*

Day 56 *Don't compare your insides to someone else's outside. ~ Ohmyhandmade.com*

Day 57

The problem with putting others first is that you've taught them you come in second.

~ Pinterest.com

Day 58

Listen to the inner wisdom of your soul and not the random opinion of others. Don't waste time living the life of others. ~ Rishi Kjain

Day 59

Wrong is wrong even if everyone else is doing it. Right is right even if you are the only one doing it.   ~ Adapted from Quotesvalley.com

Day 60

Hope is like a road in the country. There never was a road but when many walk on it, the road comes into existence.   ~ Lin Yutang

Day 61

Nobody can bring you peace but yourself.

~ Ralph Waldo Emerson

Day 62   *Instead of worrying about what you cannot control, shift your energy to what you can create.*
~ Roy T. Bennett

Day 63   *Happiness is a direction, not a place.*
~ Sidney J. Harris

Day 64 *Don't be afraid of losing people. Be afraid of losing yourself trying to please everyone around you.   ~ Pinterest.com*

Day 65

It is not selfish to love yourself, to take care of yourself and to make your happiness a priority. No it is not selfish, it is necessary.

~ Mandy Hale

Day 66

The beauty of life does not only depend on how happy you are, but also how happy others can be because of you.
~ Livelifehappy.com

____

____

____

____

____

____

____

____

____

Day 67

Your life will get better when you realize it's better to be alone than to chase people who don't really care about you. ~ *Thema Davis*

Day 68

Love who you are. Embrace who you are. Love yourself. When you love yourself, people can pick up on that; they can see confidence, they can see self esteem, and naturally, people will gravitate towards you.

~ Lilly Singh

Day 69
Routine and predictability is the soil that develops complacency.

~ Unknown Author

Day 70

Peace is the process of retraining your mind to process life as it is rather than how you think it should be.

~ Wayne Dyer

Day 71
Your vision becomes clear when you look inside your heart. Who looks outside, dreams. Who looks inside, awakens. ~ Carl Jung

Day 72

It is not joy that makes you grateful; rather, it is gratitude that makes you joyful.
~ David Steindl-Rast

Day 73 *When you have to start compromising yourself and your morals for the people around you, it's probably time to change the people around you.* ~ *Luckybannu*

Day 74 *Don't let someone dim your light simply because it's shining in their eyes.*
~ Sri Fatel

Day 75

There is a higher court than the courts of justice and that is the court of conscience. It supersedes all other courts.

~ Mahatma Gandhi

Day 76

Life is like a camera; focus on what's important, capture the good times, develop from the negatives and if things don't work out, take another shot. ~ Ziad K. Abdelnour

Day 77
Who you are tomorrow begins with what you do today.
           ~ Tim Fargo

Day 78

Happiness is the art of never holding in your mind the memory of any unpleasant thing that has passed.   ~ Howtobehappy.guru

Day 79

Don't change so people will like you. Be yourself and the right people will love the real you. ~ *Lessonslearnedinlife.com*

Day 80 *There is a dressmaker that specializes in alterations.* ~ *Faith Baldwin*

Day 81

Inner peace begins the moment you choose not to allow another person or event to control your emotions. ~ Pema Chodron

Day 82

Happiness is an inside job. Don't assign anyone else that much power over your life.

~ Mandy Hale

Day 83
You cannot solve your problems with the same thinking you used when you created them.

~ Albert Einstein

Day 84

If you cannot find peace within yourself, you will never find it anywhere else.

~ Marvin Gaye

Day 85

Be willing to walk alone. Many who started with you weren't intended to finish with you.

~ Adapted from yourquote.in

____

____

____

____

____

____

____

____

____

Day 86 *Be thankful for where you are and keep working towards where you want to go.*
~ Author Unknown

Day 87   *Don't ruin a good today by thinking about a bad yesterday. Let it go.*

~ Russell Simmons

Day 88

Day 89

Beauty is what you feel about yourself, not what you see in the mirror.

~ Pinterest.com

Day 90

If you don't like the road you're walking, start paving another one. ~ Dolly Parton

Day 91

We must be willing to let go of the life we planned so as to have the life that is waiting for us. ~ *Joseph Campbell*

Day 92

Don't wait until you've reached your goal to be proud of yourself. Be proud of every step you take toward reaching it. ~ Pinterest.com

Day 93

You alone are the judge of your worth and your goal is to discover infinite worth within yourself, no matter what anyone else thinks.
                                        ~ Deepak Chopra

Day 94

Be thankful for closed doors, detours and roadblocks. They protect you from paths and places not meant for you.   ~ Alex Rawat

Day 95
There is nothing more rare, nor more beautiful than a woman being unapologetically herself; comfortable in her perfect imperfection. That is the true essence of beauty.

~ Dr. Steve Maraboli

Day 96

It's never too late to start over. If you weren't happy yesterday, try something different today. Don't stay stuck, do better.

~ Delightfulquotes.com

Day 97

When you are comfortable in your own skin, you can be at peace anywhere.
~ Antsy McClain

Day 98
In the end, people will judge you anyway, so don't live your life trying to impress others. Live your life impressing yourself.
~ Eunice Camacho Infante

Day 99
Maturity is learning to walk away from people and situations that threaten your peace of mind, self respect, morals, values or self worth.

~ Unknown Author

Day 100 *When a train goes through a tunnel and it gets dark, you don't throw away your ticket and jump off. You sit still and trust the engineer. That's how life is. Sometimes you have to be still and trust your Engineer to get you through.*
~ Paraphrase from Corrie Ten Boom

Day 101

Being strong doesn't always mean standing your ground and fighting your battles. Sometimes just summoning the courage to walk away with your head held high and your pride intact is the greatest show of strength.

~ Adapted from Pinterest.com

Day 102

Happiness is not a checklist. A dream job, a fast car, a good home, even love means nothing if you have not yet found a way to feel full and content in your own mind and heart.

~ Beau Taplin

Day 103

What you tell yourself everyday will either lift you up or tear you down.
~ Unknown Author

Day 104

At any given moment in your life you have the power to say, "This is not how my story is going to end."

~ Hetvi

Day 105

Knowing when to walk away is wisdom. Being able to is courage. Walking away with your head held high is dignity.

~ Author Unknown

Day 106

Never let mistakes define who you are. Only you can choose who you are and who you become. ~ Quotespie.com

Day 107

The moment you feel like you have to prove your worth to someone is the moment to absolutely and utterly walk away.

~ Alysia Harris

Day 108

Success is a state of mind. If you want success, start thinking of yourself as a success.
~ *Joyce Brothers*

Day 109

Guilt is like a gauge or a light on the dashboard. It means something is wrong.

~ Wade Powers

Day 110

*It's not about being the best;
it's about being better than you were yesterday.*
~ Pinterest.com

Day 111

Most people think the worst thing in life is to be all alone, it's not. The worst thing in life is to end up with people that make you feel all alone.
　　　　　　　　~ Robin Williams

Day 112

One small crack does not mean that you are broken. It means that you were tested and you didn't fall apart. ~ Linda Poindexter

Day 113

People are like music, some speak the truth and others are just noise.

~ Bill Murray

Day 114

There are some people who always seem angry and continuously look for conflict. Walk away; the battle they are fighting is not with you. It is with themselves.

~ Author Unknown.

Day 115

The greatest challenge in life is discovering who you are. The second greatest is being happy with what you find.

~ Author Unknown.

Day 116

Accept what is, let go of what was, and have faith in what will be.

~ Pinterest.com

Day 117

The happiness in our lives depends on the totality and quality of our thoughts.

~ Slideshare

Day 118

Don't change so people will like you. Be yourself and the right people will love the real you.   ~ Rick & Susan Crawford

Day 119

When you find peace within yourself, you become the kind of person who can live at peace with others. ~ Unknown Author

Day 120

Happiness cannot be traveled to, owned, earned or won. It is the spiritual experience of living every minute with love, grace and gratitude.   ~ Denis Waitley

Day 121

If you are willing to change your thinking, you can change your life.
~ Louise Hay

Day 122

The way you treat yourself sets the standard for others on how you demand to be treated. Don't settle for anything other than respect. ~ *Boardofwisdom.com*

Day 123

Don't allow your wounds to transform you into someone you are not.
~ Themindsjournal.com

Day 124

Life is not about being dealt a good hand; it's about playing good with the hand you were dealt   ~ Paraphrase by Randy Pausch

Day 125

If you are not thankful for what you have, you probably won't be thankful for what you're going to get. ~ Frank A. Clark

Day 126

You are confined only by the walls you build yourself.   *~ Andrew Murphy*

Day 127

The more anger you hold in your heart towards the past, the less capable you are of loving the present. ~ Boardof wisdom.com

Day 128

If you don't design your own life plan, chances are you'll fall into someone else's plan...and what someone else plans for you is probably not much. Are you the driver or passenger in your own life journey?

~ Paraphrase by Jim Rohn

Day 129

The problem with guilt is that it cements you to the past. ~ Kevin Leman

Day 130

Knowledge is knowing what to say. Wisdom is knowing whether to say it or not.
~ Unknown Author

Day 131

Loneliness is an emotion and being alone can be a choice. You can be alone without feeling the loneliness. ~ Yourquote.in

Day 132

Move on. It's just a chapter in the past. Don't close the book, just turn the page. Embrace the next chapter in your life.

~ Adapted from Quotespie.com

Day 133

Don't expect to see positive changes in your life if you continuously surround yourself with negative people.

~ Quotesvalley.com

Day 134

Gratitude makes sense of our past, peace for today, and creates a vision for tomorrow.
~ Melody Beattie

Day 135

Instead of asking the Lord to bless what you are doing, ask Him to help you do what He's already blessing.

~ Unknown Author

Day 136

Get in the habit of asking yourself, "does this support the life I'm trying to create?" If it doesn't, ask yourself, "why am I doing this?" ~Adapted from Pinterest.com

____

____

____

____

____

____

____

____

Day 137 *Confusion comes when you try to convince our heads of something our spirit knows is not right.*   *~ Unknown Author*

Day 138

One small positive thought in the morning can change your whole day.

~ Unknown Author

Day 140

God gave us the gift of life. It is up to us to give ourselves the gift of living well.

~ Voltaire

Day 141

In the process of letting go, you will lose many things from the past, but you will find yourself. ~ Deepak Chopra

Day 142

This is my life...my story...my book. I will no longer let anyone write it; nor will I apologize for any edits I make.

~ Steve Maraboli

Day 143

Peace does not mean to be in a place where there is no noise, trouble or hard work. It means to be in the midst of those things and still be calm in your heart. ~ *Lady GaGa*

Day 144

You will never be happy if you constantly worry about what others think of you.
~ Idlequotes.com

Day 145

Holding on is believing that there is a past; letting go is knowing that there is a future. ~ *Daphne Rose Kingman*

Day 146

Keep away from people who try to belittle your ambition. Small people always do that, but the really creative ones make you feel that you too can become great.   ~ Mark Twain

Day 147

Be selective with your battles. Sometimes being at peace is better than being right.

~ Unknown Author

Day 148

It all begins and ends in your mind. What you give power to has power over you.
~ Leon Brown

Day 149

You may not be where you want to be, but you can look back and be thankful that you are not where you used to be.

~ Joel Olsteen

Day 150

Never be defined by someone else's opinion of you...unless they hold a higher opinion of you than you do of yourself.
~ Audrey Moralez

Day 151
Clean out your closet. Get rid of things that you will no longer wear; shame, pain, secrets and guilt.　　~ *Rhonda Gales*

Day 152

Let today be the day you give up who you've been for who you can become.

~ Hal Elrod.

Day 153

Show respect even to the people who don't deserve it; not as a reflection of their character, but as a reflection of yours.

~ Dave Willis

Day 154

Don't let the behavior of others destroy your inner peace. ~ Dalai Lama

Day 155

Life will keep bringing you the same test, over and over again until you pass it.
~ Pinaki Nayak

Day 156

The greatest discovery you can make is to realize that you can alter your life by altering your attitude. As you think, so shall you be.

~ William James

Day 157

Don't let your fear of what could happen make nothing happen.

~ Picturequotes.com

Day 158

You cannot heal the past by dwelling there; you can heal the past by living in the present.

~ Adapted from Marianne Williamson

Day 159

The painful truth about life is not death, but death while you are still alive. All death is not unto the grave.

~ Adapted from Norman Cousins

Day 160

A change of self is needed more than a change of scenery. When you change yourself, your circumstances will change.

~ Adapted from Arthur Christopher Benson

Day 161

Physical strength is measured by what you can carry. Inner strength is measured by how much you can bear.

~ Quotesvalley.com

Day 162

People only treat you one way. The way you allow them. ~ Livelifehappy.com

Day 163

We have all been placed on this earth to discover our own path and we will never be happy if we live someone else's idea of life.

~ James Van Praagh

Day 164

Your friends should be the angels that lift you up when you forget how to fly.
~ Athousandpetals.org

Day 165

The beauty of life is, while we cannot undo what is done, we can see it, understand it, learn from it and change so that every new moment is spent not in regret, guilt or anger but in wisdom, understanding and love.

~ *Jennifer Edwards*

Day 166

Your happiness can never come to you. It can only come from you.
~ Ralph Marston

Day 167

Life isn't about finding yourself. Life is about creating yourself.
~ George Bernard Shaw

Day 168

We attract the frequency that we send out. Who's in your circle?
~ Adapted from Delvewithin.com

Day 169

We are all here for some special reason. Stop being a prisoner of your past and become the architect of your future.

~ Robin Sharma

Day 170

When you force the pieces to fit the puzzle of your life, the picture is never right. Forcing something to fit doesn't make it right.

~ Paraphrase Sindi Sims

____

____

____

____

____

____

____

____

____

____

Day 171

If someone wants to be a part of your life, they'll make an effort to be in it. So don't bother reserving a space in your heart for someone who doesn't make an effort to stay.

~ Adapted from truthfollower.com

Day 172

We all feel guilty for the things we could have done better. But we need to let go of the guilt and remind ourselves to do better next time.
~ Steve Atchinson

Day 173

Day 174

Plan your work and work your plan. Put God first and your plan will always work. ~ Adapted from Napoleon Hill/Vicki Poole

Day 175

Instead of wondering when your next vacation is, try setting up a life for yourself that you don't need to escape from.

~ Seth Godin

Day 176

Ego says, "Once everything falls into place, I'll find peace." Spirit says, "Find your peace and then everything will fall into place. ~ Marianne Williamson

Day 177

You are not always able to control what goes on in your outer world, but you can always control what goes on in your mental world. ~ Roxanna Jones

Day 178

Until you are comfortable with being alone, you'll never know if you are choosing someone out of love or loneliness.

~ Mandy Hale

Day 179

No one can make you feel inferior without your permission.
~ Eleanor Roosevelt

Day 180

When thinking about life, remember this; no amount of guilt can change the past and no amount of worry can change the future.

~ Unknown Author

Day 181

The Lord will either calm your storm or allow it to rage while He calms you. Peace be still.

~ Adapted from boardof wisdom.com

Day 182

Your value does not decrease based on someone's inability to see your worth.

~ Zig Ziglar

Day 183

You were not given a good life or a bad life. You were given life. It's up to you to make it good or bad.   *~ Unknown Author*

Day 184

A bend in the road is not the end of the road unless you fail to make the turn.

~ Helen Keller

Day 185

Listen to your own voice, your own soul; too many people listen to the noise of the world instead of themselves.   ~ Shibani

Day 186

You can have anything you want if you are willing to give up the belief that you can't have it. ~ Robert Anthony

Day 187

Life only gets better when you do. Work on yourself and the rest will follow.
~ Unknown Author

Day 188

In every single thing you do, you are choosing a direction. Your life is a product of choices. ~ Dr. Kathleen Hall

Day 189

The happiness in your life depends on the quality of your thoughts.
~ *Marcus Aurelius*

Day 190

Respect people who find time for you in their busy schedules. But love people who never look at their schedules when you need them.   ~ Unknown/boardofwisdom.com

Day 191

Maybe the "good stuff" isn't ahead or behind us. Maybe it's somewhere in between. Right in the midst of this moment, here and now. ~ Jeff Goins

Day 192

Our greatest enemies, the ones we must fight most often, are within. The enemy is within me.
                    ~ Thomas Paine

Day 193

Every friend you can count is not necessarily one you can count on.

      ~ Unknown Author

Day 194

It is not joy that makes us grateful; it is gratitude that makes us joyful.
~ *David Steindl-Rast*

Day 195

There are two ways of spreading light; to be the candle or the mirror reflecting it.

~ Edith Wharton

Day 196

If you are depressed, you are living in the past. If you are anxious, you are living in the future. If you are at peace, you are living in the present.
                                        ~ Lao Tzu

Day 197

The only thing that will make you happy is being happy with who you are and not who people think you are.   ~ Goldie Hawn

Day 198

If you want peace, stop fighting. If you want peace of mind, stop fighting with your thoughts.   ~ Peter McWilliams

Day 199

No matter how many times a snake sheds its' skin, it will always be a snake. Remember that before allowing people back into your life.

~ Pinterest.com

Day 200

Forgiving yourself is just as important as forgiving others. Guilt is toxic, reliving the mistake over and over. Love yourself. Forgive yourself.   ~ Hope In Recovery

Day 201

Everyone is not going to love you and they don't have to...It is not their obligation. Learn to love and accept yourself.

~ Boardofwisdom.com

Day 202

You deserve to be happy and excited about the life you live. Don't let other people make you forget that. ~ Extramadness.com

Day 203

Fear is the darkroom where your negatives are developed. ~ Zig Ziglar

Day 204

If your compassion does not include yourself, it is incomplete.   *~ Buddha*

Day 205

Cry, forgive, learn, and move on. Let your tears water the seeds of your future happiness.
~ Steve Maraboli

Day 206

No one has power over you unless you give it to them. You are in control of your life and your choices. Decide your own fate.

~ Thegoodvibe.com

Day 207

Life is too short to spend it with people who suck the happiness out of you.

~ Steve Maraboli

Day 208

If it costs you your peace of mind, the cost is too high. ~ Unknown Author

Day 209
Sometimes in life you meet someone who you just connect with so much. It strangely feels comfortable from the start...that's when two souls synch. ~ Pinterest.com

Day 210

If you don't love what you do, you won't do it with much conviction or passion.
~ Mia Hamm

Day 211

Just because some people are fueled by drama, doesn't mean you have to attend the performance. ~ Unknown Author

Day 212

The way you treat yourself sets the standard for others on how you demand to be treated. Don't settle for anything other than respect.

~ Boardofwisdom.com

Day 213

Don't judge each day by the harvest you reap, but by the seeds you plant.
~ Robert Louis Stevenson

Day 214

Take time everyday to be thankful for everything that you have. You can always have more, but you could also have less.

~ Mohd Uved

Day 215

Don't kill someone with kindness because not everyone deserves your kindness. Kill people with silence, because not everyone deserves your attention.

~ Themindjournal.com

Day 216

Learn to admit your mistakes before someone exaggerates the story.
~ Iliketoquote.com

Day 217

____

____

____

____

____

____

____

____

Day 218

If you're not comfortable within yourself, you'll never find comfort with others.

~ *Pinterest.com*

Day 219

You cannot force someone to respect you, but you can refuse to be disrespected. ~ Boardofwisdom.com

Day 220

There are two kinds of guilt; the kind that drowns you until you're useless, and the kind that powers your soul to purpose.

~ Sabaa Tahir

Day 221

Show respect even to people who don't deserve it; not as a reflection of their character but as a reflection of yours.

~ Dave Willis

Day 222

The things we take for granted, someone else is praying for.

~ Wisdomquotes.com

Day 223

If you get to a place where nothing goes right, go left. ~ ayQuotable.com

Day 224

If you feel like there is something out there that you're supposed to be doing, if you have a passion for it, stop wishing and just do it.

~ Wanda Sykes

Day 225

Day 226

Joy comes from within and is not dependent on external circumstances. Rejoice always. ~ *Philippians 4:4*

Day 227

The way you think will change the way you feel, and the way you feel will change the way you behave. The choice is yours.

~ Heritier Ndanyuzwe

Day 228

The ones who notice the storms in your eyes, the silence in your voice and the heaviness in your heart are the ones you need to let in.

~ Steve Maraboli

Day 229

Life is not about making others happy. Life is about sharing your happiness with others. ~ *Unknown Author*

Day 230

When you accept yourself, you are freed from the burden of needing others to accept you. Don't allow anyone or anything to control, limit, repress, or discourage you from being your true self. ~ Steve Maraboli

Day 231

When things go wrong, take a moment to be thankful for the many things that are going right.   *~ Likequote.com*

Day 232

____

____

____

____

____

____

____

____

____

Day 233
It takes but one positive thought when given a chance to survive and thrive to overpower an entire army of negative thoughts. ~ *Robert J. Schuller*

Day 234

We learn something from everyone who passes through our lives. Some lessons are painful, some are pleasurable...but all are priceless. ~ Author Unknown.

Day 235

Don't rely on someone else for your happiness and self worth. Only you can be responsible for that. You have to invest in yourself or no one else will. ~ Stacey Charter

Day 236

You are not a product of your circumstances; you are a product of your decisions.
~ Stephen Covey

Day 237

Cutting people out of your life doesn't mean that you hate them. It simply means you respect yourself. Not everyone is meant to stay.

~ Lifelifehappy.com

Day 238

Don't get upset with people or situations. Both are powerless without your reaction. ~ *Wisdomlifequotes.com*

Day 239

Although time seems to fly by as we grow older, it never travels faster than one day at a time. Each day is a new opportunity to live your life to the fullest. ~ Steve Maraboli

Day 240

Every weakness you have is an opportunity for God to show His strength in your life. "My grace is sufficient for you, for My power is made perfect weakness." ~ 2Corithians 12:9

Day 241

It doesn't matter how slow you go, as long as you don't stop. ~ Confucius

Day 242

The only way to get better is to surround yourself with better people. Sometimes in life, as you grow, your friends will either grow or go. Surround yourself with people who reflect your values, goals and interests. ~ Adapted from Dr. Shaquille O'Neal

Day 243

Your life is a result of choices you made. If you don't like your life, it's time to start making better choices. ~ Author Unknown

Day 244

Be thankful for where you are and keep working towards where you want to be.

~ Thinkgrowprosper.com

Day 245

Don't make excuses, make changes.
~ Tony Horton

Day 246

Life is like riding a bicycle. To keep your balance, you must keep moving.
~ Albert Einstein

Day 247

If there is no inner peace, people can't give it to you; not your spouse, friends or children can give it to you. It is something you have to give to yourself.

~ Linda Evans

Day 248

When you compete with yourself, you become better. If you continuously compete with others, you only become bitter.

~ Emilyquotes.com

Day 249

When you focus on being a blessing, God makes sure that you are always blessed in abundance.   *~ Joel Olsteen*

Day 250

A friend is someone who knows the songs in your heart and sings it back to you when you have forgotten the words.
~ Donna Roberts

Day 251

Forgiveness is not something we do for other people. It's something we do for ourselves to move on. ~ Pinterest.com

Day 252

Never lose your dignity and self respect trying to make people love and appreciate you when they just aren't willing to.

~ Ms. Namu Thakuri

Day 253

Live your life in such a way that if anyone spoke badly of you, no one would believe them.

~ Author Unknown

Day 254

Day 255
You need people in your life that will tell you what you need to know and not just what you want to hear. ~ Linda H. Williams

Day 256

You attract what you are, not what you want. So, if you want it, reflect it.

~ Tony Gaskins

Day 257

Children are happy because they don't have a file in their minds called, "all the things that could go wrong."

~ Marianne Williamson

Day 258

Friends are the family we choose for ourselves.

~ Pinterest.com

Day 259

Forgive others, not because they necessarily deserve forgiveness, but because you deserve peace.   ~ Jonathan Lockwood Huie

Day 260

If you are trapped between your feelings and what other people think is right, always go for whatever makes you happy. Unless you want everyone to be happy except you.
~Positive Outlooks

Day 261

Don't be pushed around by the fears in your mind. Be led by the dreams in your heart.

~ Roy T. Bennett

Day 262

You have made some mistakes and you may not be where you want to be, but that has nothing to do with your future.

~ Zig Ziglar

Day 263

You can't always control who walks into your life but you can control which window to throw them out of. Everyone doesn't deserve to be in your life.   ~ *Lifehack.org*

Day 264

It's up to you to make your own history.
~ African Blessing

Day 265

Be sure everyone in your boat is rowing and not drilling holes when you're not looking. Know your circle.

~ Adapted from Steve Maraboli

Day 266

Be thankful for wrong relationships. They teach you, change you, strengthen you and prepare you for the right one.

~ Pinterest.com

Day 267

Feeling gratitude and not expressing it, is like wrapping a present and not giving it.
~ William Arthur Ward

Day 268

Stop looking for happiness in the same place you lost it.
~ Themindsjournal.com

Day 269

Everyone has the right to be happy without feeling guilty.   *~ Pinterest.com*

Day 270

Don't expect to see positive changes in your life if you surround yourself with negative people.

~ Robert Tew

Day 271

Believe with all your heart that you will do what you were made to do.

~ Orison Swett Marden

Day 272

Be thankful for closed doors, detours and roadblocks. They protect you from paths and places not meant for you.
~ Unknown Author

Day 273

Day 274

Happiness is letting go of what you think your life is supposed to look like and celebrating it for everything that it is.

~ Mandy Hale

Day 275

It is essential to know where to place people in your life. Not everyone deserves a front row seat as your story plays out. A clear understanding of who people are to you makes a healthy relationship. It's okay to cut toxic people out of your life.

~ Dorion Renaud

Day 276

When you discover your worth, you'll find it harder to stay around people who don't. ~ *Neeraj Kumar Singal*

Day 277

Don't let other people tell you how to live your life. Live your life how you see fit. Don't let them tell you how to be you. You're you, not the person they want you to become.

~ Hah Lao

Day 278

Find peace within your broken pieces.
~ Linda H. Williams

Day 279

There is no sense in punishing your future for the mistakes of your past. Forgive yourself. Grow from it and then let it go.
~ Melanie Koulouris

Day 280

Once you learn how to be happy, you won't tolerate being around people who make you feel anything less.
~ Germany Kent

Day 281

Your time here is limited, so don't waste your time living someone else's life.
~ Steve Jobs

Day 282

Live your truth. Express your love. Share your enthusiasm. Take action towards your dreams. Walk your talk. Dance and sing to your music. Embrace your blessings. Make today worth remembering. ~ Steve Maraboli

Day 283

Don't live the same year 75 times and call it life.
~ Robin S. Sharma

Day 284

You can only give your best to others when you are in touch with the best in yourself.

~ Rhythm of Life

____

____

____

____

____

____

____

____

____

Day 285

Life is too short to waste your time on people who don't respect, appreciate and value you.

~ Roy T. Bennett

Day 286

The only person you should try to be better than is the person you were yesterday.
~ Unknown Author

Day 287

Day 288

Your struggle is just a chapter in your story. It's not the ending.

~ Boardofwisdom.com

Day 289   *In order to be walked over,
you have to be lying down. Stand tall.*
~ Brian Weir

Day 290

When the wrong people leave your life, right things start happening.
~ Quotefancy.com

____

____

____

____

____

____

____

____

____

____

____

Day 291

One of the simplest ways to stay happy is…letting go of what makes you sad.

~ Raiseyourmind.com

Day 292

The person who angers you, controls you. Don't give anyone that power, especially the one who does it intentionally.

~ Dailyinspirationalquotes.com

Day 293

Be thankful for what you have; you'll end up having more. If you concentrate on what you don't have, you'll never have enough.

~ Oprah

Day 294

A man's heart plans his way but the Lord orders his steps. ~ Proverbs 16:9

Day 295

Let go of people who dull your shine, poison your spirit, and bring you drama. Cancel your subscription to their issues.

~ Steve Maraboli

Day 296

Every story has an end, but in life, every end is a new beginning.
~ Uptown Girls

Day 297

Getting knocked down in life is a given. Getting up and moving forward is a choice.

~ Zig Ziglar

Day 298

When life places a wall in your path, you have two choices. You can either beat your head against it or you can figure out a way to get around it.

~ Randi G. Fine

Day 299

Be thankful for today, because in one moment, your entire life can change.
~ Mesmerizingquotes.com

Day 300

Fear is the worst kind of grave because it buries you alive.   ~ Beth Fantaskey

Day 301

Guilt isn't always a rational thing...Guilt is a weight that will crush you whether you deserve it or not.~ Maureen Johnson

Day 302

You will get what you want when you stop making excuses on why you don't have it.
~ Rad Gamer

Day 303

Don't let people pull you into their storm; pull them into your peace.

~ Unknown Author

Day 304

Starting today, forget what's gone; appreciate what still remains and look forward to what's coming next. ~ Pinterest.com

Day 305

Self care is not selfish. You cannot serve from an empty vessel.

~ Eleanor Brown.

Day 306

If you don't see your worth, you'll always choose people who don't see it either. When your self esteem rises, your life follows.
~ Mandy Hale

Day 307

If you do not go after what you want, you'll never have it. If you do not ask, the answer will always be no. If you don't step forward, you're always in the same place.

~ Nora Roberts

Day 308
Happiness will come to you when it comes from you. Stop expecting it from someone else and begin to take responsibility for making it so.   ~ Adapted from Ralph Marston

Day 309

If you don't like where you are, change it. If you can't change the people around you, change the people you're around.
~ Adapted from Pinterest

Day 310

Saying yes to happiness means learning to say no to things and people that stress you out.
                                        ~ Thema Davis

Day 311

When someone says you've changed, it simply means you've stopped living your life their way. ~ Unknown Author

Day 312

It all begins and ends in your mind. What you give power to has power over you, if you allow it. ~ *Positive Energy*

Day 313

We make a living by what we get, but we make a life by what we give.

~ Winston Churchill

Day 314

Don't hold onto the guilt of mistakes you have made, that have kept you from moving forward. Focus on what you have learned. Forgive yourself. Today is a new day.

~ Sassy Six

Day 315

In the process of letting go, you will lose many things from the past, but you will find yourself. ~ Deepak Chopra

Day 316

Be a reflection of what you'd like in others. If you want love, give love. If you want honesty, give honesty. If you want respect, give respect. ~ *Spiritualcleansing.org*

Day 317

Day 318

People may forget what you said and they may forget what you did, but they will never forget how you made them feel.
~ Maya Angelou

Day 319

Be thankful for your struggles because without them, you wouldn't have stumbled across your strengths. ~ Alex Elle

Day 320

If you're going to stay, stay forever. If you're going to leave, then do it today. If you're going to change, change for the better. And if you're going to talk, make sure you mean what you say. ~ *Pinterest.com*

Day 321

Happiness does not depend on what you have or who you are. It relies solely on what you think.
~ *Buddha*

Day 322

If you shine your soul with the same egoless humility as the rainbow then no matter where you go in this world or the next, love will find you, attend you, and bless you.

~ Aberjhani

Day 323

Life is too short to spend it with people who suck the happiness out of you.
~ *Dreamsquote.com*

Day 324

Worrying does not take away tomorrow's troubles. It takes away today's peace.
~ Unknown Author

Day 325

Your life is your message to the world. Make sure it's inspiring.
~ Inspiredtoreality.com

____

____

____

____

____

____

____

____

____

____

Day 326

It's a new day, fresh start, fresh energy, new opportunities. Get your mind right, be thankful, be positive and start your day right.

~ Unknown Author

Day 327

Your mistakes are to help you develop your purpose, not shame and guilt.
~ Sue Fitzmaurice

Day 328

Guilt is something that some people feel when they run out of excuses for their behavior.
                                    ~ Gaius Baltar

Day 329

Choose your thoughts carefully. Keep what brings you peace, release what brings you suffering and know that happiness is only a thought away.
~ Nishan Panwar

Day 330

The tongue has no bones, but it is strong enough to break a heart and wound a fragile spirit.

~ Yami

Day 331

Life is too short to start your day with the broken pieces of yesterday. It will destroy your wonderful today and ruin your great tomorrow. ~ Spiritualcleansing.org

Day 332

To remember who you are means to forget what someone told you to be.
~ Purelovequotes.com

Day 333

Protect your peace. Remove yourself from the space of ungrateful people. Sometimes people don't learn to respect you until you're no longer around for them to disrespect you. ~ Tony A. Gaskins Jr.

Day 334

In order to love who you are,
you cannot hate the experiences that shaped you.
~ Andrea Dykstra

Day 335

Beauty is being the best possible version of yourself on the inside and out.
~ Audrey Hepburn

Day 336

One way to get better is to surround yourself with people who believe in you.
~ Thinkpositive.com

Day 337

Make sure you don't start seeing yourself through the eyes of those who don't value you. Know your worth, even if they don't.

~ Unknown Author

Day 338

You teach people how to treat you by what you allow, what you stop and what you reinforce.   ~ Tony Gaskins

Day 339

It all begins with you. If you do not care for yourself, you will not be strong enough to take care of anything or anyone in life.
~ Leon Brown

Day 340

The people in your life should be the source of reducing stress, not causing more of it.   ~ Themindsjournal.com

Day 341

Love yourself enough to never lower your standards for anyone.

~ Unknown Author

Day 342   *Sometimes your circle decreases in size but increases in value.*

~ Themindsjournal.com

Day 343

Day 344

Stress is the space between your expectations and reality. ~ Unknown Author

Day 345

There are so many people out there who will tell you that you can't. What you've got to do is turn around and say," watch me!"

~ Raiseyourmind.com

Day 346

You cannot be lonely if you like the person you are alone with. ~ Wayne Dyer

Day 347

The past has no power over the present moment.

~ Eckhart Tolle

Day 348

up eight.

Fall down seven times; Stand
~ Japanese proverb

Day 349

Your positive energy and vision must be greater than anyone's negativity. Your certainty must be greater than everyone's doubt.

~ Jon Gordon

Day 350

Let your light shine so brightly that others can see their way out of the dark.
~ Katrina Mayer

Day 351

While you are busy looking for the perfect person, you'll probably miss the imperfect person who could make you perfectly happy.

~ John Spence

Day 352

Negative emotions like loneliness, envy and guilt have an important role to play in a happy life; they're big, flashing signs that something needs to change.
~ Gretchen Rubin

Day 353

Everything in life becomes easier when you don't concern yourself with what everyone else is doing.   *~ Hplyriikz.com*

Day 354

Treat people the way you want to be treated. Talk to people the way you want to be talked to. Respect is earned, not given.
~ *Hussein Nishah*

Day 355

If you allow people to make more withdrawals than deposits in your life, you will be out of balance and in the negative. Know when to close the account. ~ *Curiano.com*

Day 356

It's your road and yours alone. Others may walk it with you but no one can walk if for you.

~ Rumi

Day 357

Don't expect people to understand your grind when God didn't give them your vision. ~ *Kushandwizdom.com*

Day 358

True freedom is understanding that we have a choice in who and what we allow to have power over us.   ~ *Meryl Streep*

Day 359

As you gain confidence in yourself, red flags are no longer red flags...they become deal breakers. ~ *Pinterest.com*

Day 360

In life, it's important to know when to stop arguing with people and simply let them be wrong.

~ Ideaspot.com

Day 361   *Your diet is not only what you ear. It's what you watch, what you listen to, what your read, the people you hang around...Be mindful of the things you put into your body, emotionally, spiritually and physically.*

~ The Minds Journal

Day 362

No matter how many times a snake sheds its' skin, it will always be a snake. Remember that before allowing people back into your life.

~ Pinterest.com

Day 363

Day 364

An apology without changed behavior is just manipulation.

~ Amazingmovement.com

Day 365

Give. But don't allow yourself to be used. Love. But don't allow your heart to be abused. Trust. But don't be naïve. Listen. But don't lose your own voice. ~ *Pinterest.com*

ABOUT LINDA

Linda has been homeless, an alcoholic, a victim of domestic violence, and hopeless. Everyone has a past. That was her past. Linda is now a Bestselling Author, Insight & Wisdom Coach, Facilitator, and a National Motivational Speaker. She uses her gifts and talents to empower and encourage women to release the chains of their past. Her passion is to influence women in such a way as to inspire them into positive action. She is a nationally sought after speaker and facilitator for seminars, workshops, support groups and church organizations.

She provides CBT based life skills classes to a local prison, and offers re-entry resources to formerly incarcerated women. Linda also provides personal and professional development to women's groups and organizations, local colleges and businesses.

Linda is the author of "Your Past Has Passed" and "There Is Life After…

She has a degree in English, a Certified Insight & Wisdom Coach and a Cognitive Behavior Therapy Practitioner.

More on Linda H. Williams

To have Linda speak to your organization about the empowerment and restoration of the human spirit or other empowerment tools email linda@lindahwilliams.com.

Linda speaks on additional topics such as:

- Junk In Your Trunk
- Life Support Success Tools
- All Godz Girlz Wear Hatz
- Are You Waiting On Your Boaz

ABOUT ANGIE

Author | Empowerment Speaker | Girlfriend's Coach

Angie is an expert rainmaker whose ability to impact change in the hearts and minds of those that she develops has made her a game changer. A true influencer, she spent over 14 years as a business leader in the financial industry.

Angie has been a Girlfriend's Action coach for over 20 years using her special gift of motivating women to discover their purpose and empowering them to be successful.

Prior to moving to the Atlanta metropolitan area, Angie served with her husband as founders of Northern New Jersey's 1st pop warner Junior Football program where she raised over 10K in less than a month. They also co-chaired Community Baptist Church of Englewood's Married Couples Ministry.

While in Atlanta Angie has self-published three (3) books, the second of which, a collaboration with seven (7) girlfriends who became new authors through her coaching. She also answered the call from women needed genuine, drama free connections with like-minded women by founding the League of Girlfriends, which has grown from 9 members to over 330 in a little more than a year.

Angie serves as President of Atlanta Women's Network, GA's 1st Business Women's networking group and on the Board for Lasting Health Impact. She is also the workshop facilitator for young girls at risk with Destiny's Daughters of Promise.

She and her husband live in Acworth, GA with the light of their life, their 11 year old son Christian aka "Smooch".

More on Angie CJ Sims

Angie is available to be hired to help you publish your book, create action in your business through one-on-one coaching, motivate your team for success or increase you Management's Diversity awareness.

She can speak to your organization on following topics:

- Developing Women into Leadership;
- How to Ask for what you Deserve;
- Mastering Relationships for Success and Sales;
- Leaders with Fire Walking followers;
- Live your Purpose NOW;
- Wake UP Girlfriend! You're missing YOU;
- Keeping God in your success

Angie is happy to customize her topics to meet your organization's needs.

If interested please visit www.acjsims.com or send an email to acjsims@gmail.com

Follow Angie on Social Media
Facebook.com & LinkedIn.com - Angela Sims
Instagram.com, Twitter.com @FindGirlfriends

Visit her websites:
www.acjsims.com
www.leagueofgirlfriends.com

www.ingramcontent.com/pod-product-compliance
Lightning Source LLC
Chambersburg PA
CBHW032039050726
47590CB00001B/60